The Combat of the Thirty

DEEDS OF ARMS SERIES

Series Editor: Steven Muhlberger, Nipissing University

This series of source readers makes available to a broad audience original accounts of famous displays of martial and chivalric prowess from the Middle Ages and early Renaissance. The books provide short, vivid introductions to particular topics and events, and can also be used in combination to look at the complex phenomenon of chivalric competition. Each volume includes a comprehensive introduction, color gallery of contemporary illustrations, and bibliography for further reading. Five volumes are currently scheduled for publication; others are under consideration.

Check our website for updates: www.freelanceacademypress.com.

DEEDS OF ARMS SERIES   VOLUME 2

The Combat of the Thirty

Translated and Edited by Steven Muhlberger

Freelance Academy Press, Inc.
www.FreelanceAcademyPress.com

Cover Illustration: La chanson de Bertrand du Guesclin (c. 1382), Yates Thompson 35, 90v, British Library. © British Museum. Used with permission.
A near contemporary depiction of the Battle of Auray (29 September, 1364). Auray proved the decisive battle of the Breton War of succession. Charles de Blois was killed in the battle, enabling Jean de Montfort to claim the Duchy without further conflict. A number of the survivors of the Combat of the Thirty took part in the fighting in Auray, including Hugh Calveley and Jehan de Beaumanoir.

Appendix 2: *Armor of the Combat of the Thirty, 1351.* © 2012 Douglas Strong

Freelance Academy Press, Inc., Wheaton, IL 60189
www.freelanceacademypress.com

Printed in the United States of America
by Publishers' Graphics

21 20 19 18 17 16 15 14 13 12   1 2 3 4 5

ISBN 978-1-937439-02-6

Library of Congress Control Number: 2012951736

Contents

List of Illustrations

1.

A Confrontation in Brittany

On March 27, 1351, sixty armed men (or, some think, sixty-two) gathered in a field in Brittany, halfway between the two enemy castles of Josselin and Ploërmel. These sixty—or rather two groups of thirty—men-at-arms represented the garrisons of those two strongholds, and they had appeared in this field, near an impressive tree later known as the Halfway Oak, to make good on a captain's promise: "We will go to an open field and there we will fight as long as we can endure it."

There was no tactical or strategic goal behind the Combat of Thirty against Thirty (usually called simply "the Combat of the Thirty"); nevertheless, the battle was fought until all on one side were dead or captured, and no one ran away, all present feeling that they "neither could nor should flee." This showdown in the fields of Brittany attracted attention in its own time and the story has been retold in many eras since. There is today a monument to the Combat, which stands where the Halfway Oak once grew, in the commune of Guillac. Was the Combat an admirable deed? Even in the fourteenth century, opinions were divided: some thought that it was a fight for no sensible reason, "the product of presumption and rashness," while others considered it a great demonstration of *prowess*, a word that designates a heroic combination of skill and courage. It is still a rare reader or listener who does not find the story fascinating when he or she first runs across it.

Why did sixty men risk themselves in a fight to the finish on that spring day in Brittany six and a half centuries ago? Why did it attract attention and praise in its time? Why does it interest us still? This introduction will try to answer these questions.

The Hundred Years War

To appreciate the Combat, some knowledge of the Hundred Years War is helpful. For English-speaking readers, the famous incidents of the war, apart from the career of Joan of Arc, are three major battles: the English victories at Crécy, Poitiers and Agincourt. Those, however, were three exceptional days out of more than a century of war. For most who experienced it, as warrior or non-combatant, the Hundred Years War was an inconclusive, shapeless thing, without set battles or organized campaigns, but no less destructive for all that.

There were two stated reasons for the conflict. The kings of England had long held the continental territory of Gascony as vassals of the King of France. The two kings' respective rights over Gascony were always a matter of dispute, and the embarrassment the English king felt about being the "man," or subject, of another ruler made disagreements hard to resolve. One such quarrel, between Edward III of England and Philip VI of France, broke into open war in 1337.

Soon after, Edward III raised a second issue, one that proved to be even harder to resolve than the status of Gascony. He declared that his rival was not rightfully King of France at all. Rather, as grandson of Philip IV, Edward was the true heir to the French throne. How sincere Edward was and how good his claim mattered less than the fact that Edward could now use the claim to political and military advantage. Any French lords whom Edward might win over to his side could maintain that they were not traitors to Philip VI, but had merely come to recognize Edward's better right to the throne. The war between the two monarchs now had the potential to become a French civil war.

And this is precisely what happened. Dissatisfied French princes and faction leaders always had a friend in Edward or his successors. Such allies made it possible for English armies to land without opposition on the continent and conduct devastating campaigns. If the French kings directly confronted the English armies, whose tactical methods were superior in this era, they risked and sometimes experienced costly defeats. If they did not fight the English, however, the French kings' practical power, prestige, and legitimacy were undermined by the fact that they were allowing their subjects to be plundered, burnt out, and killed by those who disputed their right to the throne itself.

France suffered greatly as a result. The suffering did not cease, however, when English campaigns ended, nor even when a truce was proclaimed or a peace treaty signed. Edward's attacks on France had attracted to that country a great many footloose men willing to fight for pay, the opportunity to loot, and the possibility of advancement through arms. Such men might be either noble or non-noble; no doubt in many cases their precise status was unclear. Since the practice of arms was, in theory, the monopoly of the upper class, all of them were claiming by participation in war a certain degree of social prestige. They presented themselves as men who had the right to wage war and profit from it—as "men-at-arms." The hard fact was that most of them had few better options in life than the dangerous and unhealthy pursuit of "arms." When a campaign ended or a truce was declared, they had nowhere to go. Some might be employed as garrison troops, but seldom be paid or supplied with necessities, since kings were often short of cash. In such a case, a garrison would have to tax the surrounding countryside—or plunder it, depending on one's point of view. Other warriors would have been dismissed from service and thrown to their own devices. The logical expedient for such masterless men would be to seize a strongpoint and begin taxing—or plundering—their neighbors. Whether they were acting under authority or taking matters into their own hands, the results were much the same. France was infested with a variety of war bands, which competed for the right to live off the land. One of the earliest regions to be subjected to this kind of occupation was Brittany.

Brittany

Brittany was one of the largest and most independent of the fiefs of the French crown. Located close to the French heartland and on the sea-route between England and English Gascony, it had strategic importance. In the earliest stages of the war, Duke John III of Brittany was careful to maintain neutrality, but when he died in 1341, his lack of an undoubted heir turned Brittany into a battleground. John's half-brother, John de Montfort, claimed the duchy, as did the old duke's niece, Jeanne de Penthièvre, who transmitted her right to her husband, Charles of Blois. The feuding monarchs each chose a candidate: Philip supported Charles of Blois, while Edward recognized John de Montfort as duke in return for acknowledgement that he was the true king of France.

In the years between old Duke John's death and 1347, partisans of either side ravaged Brittany. The war not only had a deleterious effect on the duchy, but also undermined the contending parties. John de Montfort spent the years 1341–5 in French captivity, and then, soon after winning his freedom, died. His few remaining supporters would have given up if his wife, Jeanne de Flandres, and his young heir, John IV, had not continued to receive English support. Charles of Blois also enjoyed his share of bad luck. In the summer of 1347 his forces lost a bloody battle at La Roche-Darrien; many of his key supporters were killed, and Charles and many others were captured and held for ransom. Charles was whisked off to England, where he was held until 1352, when he abandoned his alliance with France. Without his leadership in the field, Blois' supporters had no chance to take advantage of the weakness of his enemies. The Breton war became a standoff between the forces of "the two ladies," John's wife Jeanne de Flandres and Charles' wife Jeanne de Penthièvre, neither of whom was in a position to take the initiative.

Brittany was now a patchwork divided between garrisons supposedly supporting Montfort or Blois, England or France. This situation was unlikely to end unless one of the two kings made conquering the duchy his priority. But neither did. Edward, after his great victory at Crécy and his occupation of Calais, had bigger goals in mind. As long as his Breton garrisons kept the French from threatening the sea-lanes to Gascony, he need give no thought to that front. Philip, quite realistically, saw the scattered English forces in Brittany as the least of his problems.

Who was interested in Brittany? First, there were the native inhabitants, who were mostly concerned with defending themselves. Second, there were a large number of adventurers, some Breton, but mostly English, German, Dutch, and other foreigners, who saw the disturbed conditions as an opportunity to make a living or, perhaps, even a fortune. A man who was of no particular standing at home, if he were both ruthless and able to rally others around him, might make himself lord of a district and line his pockets with the unwilling contributions of its inhabitants. A famous instance of this is Hugh Calveley, a minor landowner from the backwoods English county of Cheshire, who, as Jonathan Sumption tells us, began accumulating his fortune in Brittany in the late 1340s, as the leader of a small group, no more than fifteen men-at-arms, drawn from among his friends and relatives. Another success story was Croquart, a German or a Dutchman who had been a page back home, but who in Brittany had made himself a rich captain. It is worth noting that both of these men fought on the "English" side at the Combat of the Thirty.

What We Know About the Combat

Our knowledge of any historic event depends on witnesses or sources who only tell us part of the story; the part that they thought was interesting. We are fortunate to have more than one account of the Combat, but this fact means we have several somewhat contradictory views of what happened and what the Combat meant. Two accounts were written close to the event. One was written by a well-known and respected Flemish chronicler named Jean le Bel. (The more famous chronicler Jean Froissart used Le Bel as the source for his somewhat later version. It seems unlikely that Froissart had any independent information about the Combat.) The second version, *The Battle of the Thirty English and the*

Thirty Bretons, was created by an anonymous Breton poet, about the same time that Le Bel wrote. These two accounts are included in this book because each gives a detailed view of the battle at the Halfway Oak.

The two writers present a very similar picture. They agree that the Combat was the result of an agreement between the captains of two garrisons, a pro-English, pro-Montfort one at Ploërmel, and a pro-French, pro-Blois one at Josselin, eight miles away. The "English" captain, Brandebourch (Brandenburgh?) or Brambrocc may or may not have been English himself; Le Bel says he was a German. In any case, his garrison was mainly made up of Englishmen and other foreigners. The "French" captain, Sir Jean de Beaumanoir (mistakenly called "Robert de Beaumont" by Le Bel) led a group of Bretons, men who were his relatives and men of some standing. Some words passed between Beaumanoir and the "English" commander and they agreed to fight a combat of thirty against thirty. An unspecified number of days later, the two captains met, accompanied by their chosen companions. As Sumption points out, there is reason to think that on each side the combatants were drawn from all over Brittany, and not exclusively from the original garrisons. Men like Croquart were there for pleasure of combat, or the opportunity to increase their reputations. The battle, which was fought mainly on foot, lasted a good long time; in fact, the combatants exhausted themselves and agreed to a break to rest, tend their wounds, and have a drink. Afterwards, the fight began to go against the English. The decisive moment came when a man-at-arms from the French side mounted a horse (or perhaps was already mounted) and used it to break up the English formation. After that, the battle quickly came to an end. A number of the English were killed, including their leader; all the rest were taken captive, according to normal fourteenth-century usage. No one ran away.

There are a couple of important differences between these accounts. The anonymous poet saw the incident as a patriotic battle between good Bretons (supporters of the French king, but not Frenchmen themselves), defending their homeland against English intruders—men who were tough warriors but not otherwise admirable. Indeed, the poet says that Beaumanoir came to Ploërmel to upbraid the English for their unjust oppression of the countryside. When his opponent rejected his complaints, Beaumanoir challenged them to an even fight, which the English commander accepted.

In Jean le Bel's telling, the behavior of the English towards non-combatants is not an issue. Beaumanoir, crossing the territory dominated by Ploërmel found himself unopposed. He decided to provoke the English captain by proposing a joust with sharp weapons between three champions on either side. The implication was that it would be a cowardly act to refuse to come out, there and then. Brandebourch or Brambrocc, who was likely Beaumanoir's social inferior (it is not clear that he was a knight or even a squire), rejected the initial challenge (did he doubt his jousting skills, or those of his men?) but refused to be shamed. It was he who proposed a bigger, longer fight, one that would prove more about their respective worth than a quickly-concluded joust. Le Bel presents the two companies, despite differences in rank, as equally admirable, equally determined to demonstrate prowess. Where the anonymous Breton poet sees this as a Breton victory upholding the cause of France, Le Bel sees it as a deed that transcends mere partisanship.

Many who have read about the Combat ask a question that these two writers leave unresolved. When the French warrior, Guillaume de Montauban, used a horse to run down the English and break up what had been a tight, effective defensive formation, was he fighting fair? The poet shows a battle which except at the very conclusion was fought on foot; in the French wars armored men-at-arms were increasingly fighting as infantry as the English showed how effective such tactics could be, even against the best cavalry. The poet dramatically tells his audience that the horse was introduced into the fight out of desperation, and at the initiative of one man. The poet has no doubt that this was a clever and admirable expedient against an enemy, and he gives no hint that using it broke any specific agreement. Although Jean le Bel also says nothing about an agreement on tactics, he may have had his doubts. He indicates that some witnesses reported that four or five Frenchmen stayed on horseback from the beginning, but that he is not sure about the truth of it. If he felt that bringing in a horse to decide the fight was somewhat dicey, he may have been trying to recast the story to account for its presence in a way that would not discredit the whole deed.

What Contemporaries Thought of the Combat

The Combat of the Thirty against Thirty went unremarked in English chronicles. Several French writers included reports (most of them quite short) in their histories. Frenchmen, in an era when French victories were scarce, had far more to gain from telling the story than the English, who could point with pride to the major battles of Sluys, Crécy, and Poitiers.

The longest and most partisan version is the *Battle of the Thirty English and the Thirty Bretons.* It is a celebration not so much of a French victory, but a Breton one, and the poem is aimed at a hometown crowd. The poet has a profound local knowledge of the event and its participants, and is especially well-informed about the Breton champions and their families. He is writing to show how certain named individuals stood up for the honor of Brittany and defeated a brutal, arrogant band of foreign plunderers. He portrays several heroes of the tale and a few of the villains as distinct personalities, and reports their words at length—boasts, invocations of God and the saints, reassurances, threats. Today's reader almost believes that this is how it really was, and the tale must have been very stirring to people who actually knew the participants.

There has always been, however, a non-partisan aspect to the tale. It is best seen in the versions of Jean le Bel and Jean Froissart (not included here since Froissart follows Le Bel's account so closely). The Combat could be, and was, seen as an example, good or bad, of how real warriors should conduct themselves. It is worth taking a moment to look at Froissart's summing up of contemporary opinion: "Some people regarded it as an affair of prowess, others as the product of presumption and rashness." Presumption or arrogance had several aspects, but perhaps the relevant meaning here is "overreaching oneself." Probably those who criticized the combatants aimed their chief barbs at those who risked themselves, for no clear reason, and then lost. Much the same criticism, however, could have been aimed at the victorious side. We know from a variety of sources that military discipline had its champions in the fourteenth century, who believed that self-will and lack of discipline among "men-at-arms" were the chief cause of the ills of the time.

Those interested in talking about the Combat, however, took a more positive view, believing it to be an example of determination and courage well beyond the ordinary, one that deserved to be remembered forever. Why? Key to the self-worth of the man-at-arms was his willingness to take on an "enterprise" (*emprise*) and fulfill it: to be as good as his word, despite all danger. Medieval warfare was a bloody affair, where most combat was face-to-face. Those few men able to keep going despite the danger of death or mutilation were greatly admired. It was such men who made the difference between victory and defeat for their side; moreover, it was such men who led companies and armies. Warriors fought fear before they faced any human enemy, and admired fearlessness in their leaders and companions even more than tactical skill. Men who sought to lead troops into battle needed a reputation for courage. That is why the English side at the Combat, for instance, included men who had retinues of their own, and wished to advance their fortunes further. To take part in a fierce "feat of arms," was not a whim, but the exploitation of an opportunity.

Determination and courage were perennial virtues, but in the 1340s and 1350s they were particularly on the minds of Frenchmen who followed the wars. The disaster of Crécy (1346) preceded the Combat of 1351. The French attacked the English boldly, but when repeated charges proved inadequate, many of them fled. Their defeat by a numerically inferior army brought down torrents of denunciation on the heads of the French king and his nobility, whose claim to power rested on their right and duty to wage war effectively. The behavior at the Combat of rather obscure Breton knights and squires, or of the more obscure mercenaries on the other side, was an object lesson in what real warriors were capable of. Such a contrast was perhaps not completely fair, but it is understandable. Only a few years later after the Combat, the

French defeat at Poitiers, complete with shameful retreat, cast the admirable qualities of the Combat and the Combatants into even higher relief, and no doubt gave new life to the story.

Certainly no one's reputation seems to have been harmed, even by having been a loser. Two of the English participants, Hugh Calveley and Robert Knolles, were among the most successful captains in the first half of the Hundred Years War. Calveley eventually gained enough wealth and renown to be a suitable match for an Aragonese princess, while Knolles gained even more success, if anything: in 2000, the *Sunday Times of London*, in a historic listing of Britain's wealthiest, named him as one of the twenty richest Britons since 1066. At the Combat both men were near the beginning of their careers, and it is not fanciful to see their participation as significant step in advancement, even if they had to pay ransoms to their Breton captors. It did not hurt them in the slightest to be known as men who, on a famous occasion, fulfilled their commitment and refused to flee.

A passage in Jean Froissart's *Chronicle* shows how the legend grew. In about 1374, the chronicler met a famous Combatant (or was it more than one?) and was very impressed:

> I saw sitting at the table of King Charles of France a Breton knight who had been there, Sir Yvain Charruel; he had a face so cut and hacked up that it really showed how well the affair had been fought. And also present was Sir Enguerrand d'Eudes, a good knight of Picardy, who showed well that he had been there, and another good squire named Hues de Raincevaux.

We feel Froissart's awe, as he meant us to; but it is interesting to note that, if the Breton poet's full list of participants is accurate, neither Enguerrand d'Eudes nor Hues de Raincevaux were present at the Combat! We can only speculate about why Froissart was told that they were.

The Lasting Impression

It is probably accurate to say that the Combat's reputation in later times has continued to have two lines of development: its reputation in Brittany and its reputation elsewhere. The Breton line followed the anonymous poet in identifying the Combat as a great patriotic victory, and the specific participants as heroes whose fame should be kept alive for posterity. Participation of an ancestor was a point of pride for their descendants.

In the eighteenth and early nineteenth century, the meaning of the Combat became controversial again, but on new grounds. Brittany was one of the French provinces most split between revolutionary radicals and aristocratic conservatives, and only the latter party claimed this event for its own. During the revolutionary Year II (1793–4), the cross that had long ago replaced the Halfway Oak as a memorial to the Combat was knocked down by republicans. Even before the Napoleonic era was over, however, leading Bretons were agitating to have the monument restored, as recalling an event much to the honor of the "Breton nation." It is probably no coincidence that the Breton nation and the rest of France were in the midst of a long war with the people across the Channel. Though that war was lost a few years later, enthusiasm for the project grew. On July 11, 1819, the reconstruction of the monument began with a great ceremony presided over by members of the local nobility and the Bishop of Vannes. The bishop gave a rousing speech about the role of religion and honor in upholding the French monarchy, and the Combat as a symbol of Brittany's participation in that grand tradition; the speech and a long list of prominent attendees can be found in the back of Crapelet's 1827 edition of the poetic account. We can wonder whether the entire crowd present was equally enthusiastic about the Combat and the way it was being used to assert eternal Breton loyalty to France and the Bourbon dynasty. A Web search today shows that it still has different resonances for different Bretons: some think it a point of local or regional pride, while others think entirely too much has been made of it over the years.

It is safe to say that in Brittany the Combat will always have a special significance it cannot have in other countries. Nevertheless, the story is well known
elsewhere, as an example of a kind of courage and chivalry specific to the time of
the Combat but having, perhaps, universal significance. Jean le Bel was the first
to write in this tradition. He believed that the Combat "should never be forgotten," as did his enthusiastic follower Jean Froissart, and each of them played their
part in memorializing it. Before a century had gone by, it had become possible to
improvise on the story as a musician might improvise on a well-known theme.
The last of the accounts translated here is an interesting reinterpretation by a Scottish chronicler, Androw of Wyntoun. Wyntoun was a high-ranking monk who
in the 1420s wrote a long verse chronicle from Creation until his own time. The
more recent parts of this *Orygynal Cronykil of Scotland* were devoted to Scottish
history, for which Wyntoun's work is most valuable; however, he did not hesitate
to add other material that caught his fancy. Wyntoun had an interest in formal
deeds of arms, and he included the Combat of the Thirty against Thirty in the
Orygynal Cronykil. He seems to have had access to the Breton poem, because
he preserves several details found there, like the use of a hammer by one of the
English combatants. Nevertheless, he felt quite free to alter even the most basic
facts. His combat, for instance, took place in Normandy rather than Brittany.
The meaning of the story he gives is also his own invention. For Wyntoun, the
Combat of the Thirty was a timeless myth of chivalry, which he felt justified in
adapting to suit his own ideas of right conduct by men-at-arms.

This introduction should probably end with some short discussion of the
Combat's significance in modern times. One hesitates, simply because there are
always, in any era, almost as many opinions as there are people. It is probably fair
to say that outside of Brittany and France the Combat is emerging from an era
of obscurity. Until quite recently, it was difficult to find an English translation of
any fourteenth-century version of the Combat, or even a detailed discussion by
a modern scholar. A few years ago, when I was asked by a major film studio to
provide them with a translation of Froissart's account, I found it hard to put my
hands on one. Although the film studio's interest soon waned, it helped awaken my

own. As I looked more closely into the matter I found that there were many people who wanted to know more about the incident. This is a great era of medieval re-enactment and re-creation, and we are going through a revival in military history, even among professionals who until recently kept their distance from the detailed investigation of war. When war and heroism are matters of public concern, the Combat of the Thirty against Thirty is a natural subject for reconsideration, and renewed debate about what is "presumption" and what is "prowess."

The Translated Texts

All three texts here were translated by me, although I have benefited from the advice of a number of helpful friends and colleagues. Josh Mittleman made suggestions about how the arms of the participants might be blazoned in English, while Dr. Elizabeth Ewan of the University of Guelph generously answered questions on Wyntoun's language. Errors, of course, are my responsibility alone.

The original text of Jean le Bel's account may be found in Jules Viard and Eugène Déprez's 1904 edition, *Chronique de Jean le Bel*, v. 2, pp. 194–7.

In translating the *Battle of the Thirty English and the Thirty Bretons*, I have followed H.R. Brush's edition in volumes 9 and 10 of the journal *Modern Philology*. There are two manuscripts of the poem, and Brush presented both facing each other. I primarily used the Bigot manuscript text but included some material that is preserved only in the Didot version (such as section V). I know of, and have consulted, two other translations, a French one in Crapelet's *Le Combat de trente Bretons contre trente Anglois* (first published in 1827), and an English one by Ainsworth in the magazine *Bentley's Miscellany* (1859).

Androw of Wyntoun's version of the story can be found in the original fifteenth-century Scots in David Laing's edition of *The Orygynale Cronykil of Scotland* (1872), v. 2, pp. 488–94.

As of this writing, the original texts of Le Bel and Wyntoun can be found at my Deeds of Arms website, as can Ainsworth's translation of the anonymous poetic account. The current address is: www.nipissingu.ca/department/history/muhlberger/chroniqu/texts/deedsch.htm.

2.

Jean le Bel's Account

How thirty French fought against thirty English and Germans by certain agreements in Brittany, and the English and the Germans were defeated.

In this same season, there took place in Brittany a most marvellous deed of arms, which should never be forgotten. And so that you are better able understand the situation, you should know that there was constant war in Brittany between the parties of the two ladies, and that Sir Charles de Blois was imprisoned in England, and although there were truces between the kings, the parties of the two ladies made war on each other.

Sir Robert de Beaumont, a valiant knight of a great family in Brittany, was castellan of Castle Josselin, where he had a great many men-at-arms and squires of his lineage. And it so happened one day that he came near the castle of Ploërmel, whose castellan was a German mercenary called Brandebourch, who had with him a great many German, Breton, and English mercenaries, and he was of the party of the Countess.

When Sir Robert saw that none of the garrison was coming out, he went to the gate and called out this Brandebourch, under a guarantee of safety, and asked him whether he had any companion, or perhaps two or three, who wished to joust with steel lances against three, for the love of their ladies. Brandebourch replied and said to him, that their lady loves would hardly wish that they should get themselves killed in a single joust, for this kind of venture was over too soon, and in it one got more of a reputation for presumption and folly than for honor and worth.

"But I will tell you what we will do. If you like, you will choose twenty or thirty of your companions from your garrison, and I will choose as many from ours and we will go to a field where no one will be able to disturb or prevent us, and command on pain of the noose to all of our companions on either side, and all those who watch us, that none should give the combatants reinforcement or help."

"By my faith," replied Sir Robert, "I agree to thirty against thirty, and I swear it thus by my faith."

"I, too," said Brandebourch, "swear it, for he who carries himself well there will gain more honor than in a joust." And so this affair was agreed and an appointment was made for the following Wednesday, four days hence.

During that time, each party chose their own thirty, just as they wished, and each of the sixty procured such armor for himself as he was able.

When the day had come, the thirty companions of Brandebourch heard Mass and then armed themselves and left for the field where the battle was to take place. And they dismounted and ordered all those who were there that none of them should be so bold as to intervene for any reason whatever.

Those thirty companions whom we will call "the English" waited a long time for those whom we will call "the French."

When the thirty French had come, they dismounted and commanded just as the English had done, that no one should give them help or aid. Some say that four or five of the French remained on horseback at the entrance to the field, and that twenty-five dismounted, just as the English had; but I don't know for certain, for I wasn't there. However it was, they spoke a little, all sixty of them, and then stepped back, each party to its own side, and made all their people retreat well back from the field.

Then one of them gave a signal and immediately they ran over and fought powerfully all in a pile, rescuing one another nobly when they got turned around and in trouble.

Soon after they had come together, one of the Frenchmen was killed, but the others did not leave off fighting on this account, but they held themselves as valiantly on both sides as if they had been all Roland or Olivier. I do not know enough to say truthfully if one side did better than the other, but they fought so long that they all lost strength and the ability to fight, due to lack of breath; it seemed a good idea for them to rest by mutual agreement. At this point there were dead one of the Frenchman and two of the English. They rested a long time, and those who had it drank some wine, and they tightened their armor which had broken and washed their wounds.

When they had rested enough, the first who got up made a sign and called the others. The battle recommenced and it lasted a long time. But in the end the English were worsted; for so I heard tell from those who were there. One of the Frenchmen who was on horseback split them up and badly trod them underfoot, so that Brandebourch their captain and eight of their companions were killed there, and the others were taken captive; when they saw that their resistance could not help them, it only remained for them to surrender or die, for they neither could nor should flee.

The same Sir Robert and his companions who remained alive took them and led them to Castle Josselin with great joy, but they left at that place, dead, six of their companions, and then many of the others died because of the wounds they had suffered.

I have not heard ever before speech or story in which such a warlike enterprise was fulfilled or went further than this one. So they who remain from this battle ought to be more honored, everywhere they go. This was in the year of grace 1351.

3.

An Anonymous Poet's Account: *La Bataille de trente Anglois et de trente Bretons*

Here commences the story of the battle of thirty English and thirty Bretons which took place in Brittany in the year of grace 1350 on the Saturday before *Laetare Jerusalem* [in our current calendar, March 27, 1351].

I

Lords, knights and barons, bannerets and bachelors,
And all noble men, pay heed to me now!
Bishops and abbots, men of religion
Heralds and minstrels, and all good companions
Gentlemen and bourgeois of all nations
Listen to this story which I wish to tell.

It is a true history, and the story a good one
About how thirty Englishmen, all bold as lions
One day fought thirty Bretons.
And I wish to tell you the truth of it, all the reasons
So that gentlefolk and clerics will often enjoy it
In their homes, a hundred years from now.

II

All good folk of honor and learning
Devote their minds, hearing and singing,
To worthy stories which lead to wisdom,
But false and jealous ones do not want to hear them at all.
Now I wish to commence and recount
That noble battle, the one called the "The Thirty."
And pray to God who allowed His flesh to be betrayed
That he will have mercy on those who fought,
Most of whom are now dust.

III

It was when Dagworth was dead, and left this earthly existence
When his life had ended before the stronghold of Auray,
At the hands of the barons of Brittany and their companies—
God give them mercy by His holy pity!
While he lived he had strictly commanded
That his English should not harm or take
The small folk of the towns and those who raise the grain.
When that baron was dead it was all forgotten.
Brambroc, who succeeded him, swore by St. Thomas
To avenge him and swept over the land.
He spoiled the country and seized Ploërmel
With grief and shame.

So he had his will in Brittany, until the day

Determined by God, when Beaumanoir the good

Who was of such renown, Sir Jean the wise

The strong and the prudent, went to the English

To parley a truce.

Thus the Bretons saw the small folk suffer,

And for them they had great pity.

One was in shackles, another was put in irons,

One in handcuffs and another in dungeon.

Two by two, three by three, each one was bound

Like cows and oxen which are led to market.

When Beaumanoir saw them his heart sighed,

And this is what he said, with great boldness to Brambroc.

"Knights of England, you do great evil,

To torment the poor people, those who sow the grain

And provide the meat and the wine that they raise.

Without such workers, nobles would have to labor

In the fields with the flail and the hoe.

They would suffer poverty, and this would be

A great and unaccustomed toil.

Those who have endured so much should have peace

From now on.

The last will of Dagworth—how soon it is forgotten!"

And Brambroc thus replied with great ferocity.

"Beaumanoir, be silent, there is nothing to discuss.

Montfort will be duke of this noble duchy,

From Pontorson to Nantes and right up to St. Mahé.

Edward will be crowned king of France,

The English have the mastery

Despite all the French and all their allies."

And Beaumanoir replied, with great civility,

"Dream another dream, this one is badly dreamed.
Never in this way will you gain half a foot."

IV

"Brambroc," said Beaumanoir, "Know for certain
That all your boasts will avail you nothing.
Those who say the most, in the end, deceive themselves.
Now please, Brambroc, let us do the smart thing.
Let us get together to fight, by appointment,
With sixty companions, or eighty or a hundred,
And then indeed we will see for truth and for a certainty,
Who will have wrong or right, without further ado."
"My lord, " this Brambroc said, "I swear it to you!"

V

"Brambroc," says Beaumanoir, "for the sake of God the just,
You are a valiant man and a very shrewd warrior,
Come on that day without asking for delay
In a year one says many a word which one wishes to recall,
And one often makes great boasts over dinner.
Do not do to me what you did to Pierre Angier
That valiant, noble man, that gentle bachelor.
He chose a day for battle with you
At the town of Ambissat. And I have heard said
That he went to that place to acquit his oath
With twenty-six spurred knights
All accoutered in gold and steel.
And Brambroc, you defaulted. You did not dare to go.
This deed we are discussing is a very great one.
You should not mock it!

People will speak of it for a very long time!"
"Beaumanoir," says Brambroc, "For God's sake let be!
For I will certainly be the first on the field.
With me will be thirty men, no more, no less,
Who will all be covered in good iron and steel.
I will not bring any villein, God give me aid!
The least of them will be a squire,
Bearing a coat of arms on his chest."
But Brambroc lies to conceal his plan,
So you do not imagine that he will bring
A bastard villein vagabond
Strong enough to carry, easily, a setier of beans
Over his neck, whose stomach was bigger
Than that of a courser. Brambroc, by his great fierceness,
Armed him this day. Through him he thought
To avenge Dagworth, when he should have struck down
Such a villein deceiver.

I now will tell you of the noble Beaumanoir.
To Brambroc he says, "I wish concerning this to go
To castle Josselin, to muster my men."
"You go," Brambroc told him. "I also wish to issue my orders
Through all the duchy. I will assemble all
The noble English I can find."

Thus was the battle vowed, that without cheating or fraud
They should fight it out in good faith
And on either side, all would be on horseback.
Pray then to the King of Glory, who knows and sees all,
That he will help those who have the right,
For this is the point at issue.

VI

At Ploërmel, now, they have sworn to do battle.

Each one has his retinue of thirty companions.

Then Beaumanoir, with an assured countenance,

Returned to Castle Josselin to tell the news.

He has no need to conceal the deed and the enterprise

Which he has arranged with Brambroc

At Ploërmel he finds a great many barons assembled

Each has given great thanks to the mercy of God.

VII

"My lords," says Beaumanoir, "you should know without delay,

That Brambroc and I have made an agreement

Of thirty companions, each one of great prowess.

So each ought to choose well those who can strike skillfully

with a lance, an axe and a heavy dagger.

So pray to the King of Glory, the God of Wisdom

That we shall have the advantage, nor should we doubt it.

They will speak of it enough in the realm of France

And through all the lands from here to Plaisance."

VIII

The noble barons have said to Beaumanoir,

What the chivalry, foot soldiers, and squires have said, too.

"We will go willingly to destroy Brambroc and all his soldiers,

And never will he have ransom or deniers of gold from us!

For we are hardy, valiant, and loyal,

We will strike the English with many great blows.

IX

Take those who please you, most noble baron!"

"I take Tinténiac, whom God bless,

And Guy de Rochefort and Charruel the Good,

Guillaume de la Marche will be my companion

And Robin Raguenel called 'of St. Symon.'

Caro de Bodegat, who ought not to be forgotten

Sir Geffroi du Bois, of great renown.

And Olivier Arrel, the hardy Breton

Sir Jehan Rousselot, who has the heart of a lion.

If these can't defend themselves from the felon Brambroc

Then I never will have any joy of my hopes."

X

"Now I ought to choose some very noble squires.

And I choose first Guillaume de Montauban

And Alain de Tinténiac, who is so good and fierce

Tristan de Pestivien, who's done so much worth praising

Alain de Keranrais and his uncle Olivier

Louis de Guyon who will come and strike with a blade of steel.

Add to him Fontenoy to test their strength.

Huet Catus the wise ought not to be forgotten

And Geffroi de la Roche who will soon be made knight;

If God please, the battle ought to remind him

Of the virtue of his father De Brice

Who campaigned all the way to Constantinople

To gain great honor.

If those can't defend themselves well against

Brambroc the tradesman, who defies Brittany—

God hinder him!—

Never ought they gird on a blade of steel!"

XI

Beaumanoir has chosen, just as I have told you,

Geffroi Poulart, Maurice de Trézéguidy, and

Guyon de Pont Blanc should not be forgotten

And Morice du Parc, a bold squire

And Geffroi de Beaucors, who was his good friend

And also the one from Lanlop, Geffroi Moelon.

All those he had named thank him,

They are all present, and bow to him.

XII

Afterwards Beaumanoir certainly takes

Jehannot De Serrant, Guillaume de la Lande.

Olivier Monteville, a man of great prowess

And Simon Richard who will not fail him there.

All put their heart and bodies in the balance.

May God preserve them from evil pestilence!

XIII

Now Beaumanoir has chosen his whole number,

Thirty good Bretons, now may God preserve them from shame.

And to their enemies let God send such an encounter

In which they will be defeated

Before the eyes of all the world.

XIV

Sir Robert Brambroc has chosen for his part

Thirty companions of whom he has great need.

I will give their names by the body of St. Bernard.

They were Knolles, Calveley, and Croquart,

Sir Jean Plesanton, Richard le Gaillard,

Helecoq his brother, and Jannequin Taillard,

Repefort-le-Valliant, Richard de la Lande

Thomelin Belifort, cunning as a fox,

Who fought with an iron hammer

Which indeed weighed twenty-five pounds,

God help me!

Hucheton de Clamaban fought with a fauchard,

With a blade on one side and hooks on the other.

It was as sharp as a dart on the point, and

Resembled the arms of King Agapart

When he long ago fought against Renouart.

When he struck a blow, the soul left the body.

Jannequin de Betonchamp, Renequin Hérouart

And Gaultier L' Alemand, Hulbure the Old.

Hennequin the Marshal, Thomelin Hualton,

Robinet Melipart, Isinnay the Hardy, Helichon the Fool,

Troussle, Robin Adés and Dango the Fleet,

Dagworth the nephew, fierce as a leopard,

And four Bretons, by the body of St. Godart

Perrot de Commellan, Guillemin the Strong,

Raoulet d'Aspremont and D'Ardaine.

They say they will defeat the Bretons, by their skill

And conquer Brittany up to Dinart.

But a fool is always a vain boaster!

XV

Now Robert Brambroc has chosen his companions,

There were thirty of them, from three different nations.

For twenty were English, bold as lions,

And six good Germans and four Bretons.

They were armed in plate, in bascinets and habergeons,

They bore swords and dag(ger)s and lances and falchions,

And the English swore to God Who suffered the Passion

That Beaumanoir the noble and good should die.

But he, the preux and wise made his devotions,

Had masses said and made great oblations

That God should give him aid through His Holy Names.

XVI

When the time had passed and the day was come

When they ought to present themselves on the grassy meadow,

Beaumanoir the valiant, whom God increases in strength,

Calls his companions. They all will come to him,

and have had masses said for them.

And each one was absolved and took the sacrament

In the name of King Jesus.

XVII

"My lords," said Beaumanoir, with his bold countenance,

"I have found the English to be of great courage.

They have a will to do us harm.

So take and demand of yourselves good courage,

Hold yourselves, each one, as valiant and prudent men.

If Jesus Christ gives you strength and the advantage

All the barons of France will take joy from it

And the debonair duke, to whom I have sworn homage

And the noble duchess who is of my lineage

Will love us always in their time."

And each one swore by God

Who made men in His image,

"If we find Brambroc in the plain, outside the bocage

Never will anyone of his lineage come back to him."

XVIII

Now I speak of Brambroc who has succeeded

In collecting thirty companions for himself.

He assembles them nobly right at the field

And tells them, in utter truth

"I have read my books, Merlin has promised

That we will have victory over the Bretons today

And then Brittany and France will belong to the good king,

Edward, for I have resolved upon it."

XIX

"My lords," says Brambroc, "Be happy and cheerful,

be certain and sure,

That Beaumanoir will be taken, him and his companions,

Hardly a one will remain alive,

And those we will bring along to the noble Edward,

Who has sent us here.

He will do to their bodies whatever he wishes

We will give back to him the lands we take

All the way to Paris.

Then we will no longer expect any Bretons to face us."

Thus spoke Brambroc according to his opinion

But if it pleases God, king of Paradise,

Let us not such a captain succeed in his plans.

XX

Now this is what Brambroc has done, and he has arrived first

With thirty companions at the grassy meadow.

In a loud voice he cries, "Beaumanoir, where are you?"

I believe indeed that you have defaulted,

But if we had joined battle, you would have done nothing."

As he spoke these words, Beaumanoir arrived.

XXI

"Beaumanoir, my friend," says Brambroc, "If you wish,

Let us put back this day to a later one,

And I will send news to noble Edward,

And you will go speak to the king of St. Denis.

And if what we have undertaken pleases them,

We will return here on a day we will set."

"My lord," says Beaumanoir, "I will take advice about this."

XXII

Beaumanoir of the steadfast mien has given the news

To the men who were present. "My lords, Brambroc wishes

To delay the thing so that each one of us

Should go without striking a blow.

Please give me your thoughts, for by that same God

Who made heaven and the dew.

For my part, I would not take all of the gold in the land

To prevent this from being fought to the finish."

Then spoke Charruel, whose color has changed.

There was no better than he from here to the salt sea.

"Lord, we are thirty who have come to this meadow

There is not of us who has not a dag, a lance, and a sword.

All of us are ready in the name of St. Honoré
To fight Brambroc, since he has challenged the noble
And debonair duke for the land.
Let him perish who leaves without striking a blow
Or who wishes to delay it to another day."
Then replied Beaumanoir, "I agree with this.
Let us go to battle as it has been sworn."

XXIII

"Brambroc," says Beaumanoir, "You will hear my intention.
See there Charruel with the bold visage and all the companions,
Who think it disgraceful that you should delay
The battle which you have offered as an outrage
To the noble duke, who is courteous and wise.
So each one swears to God Who made man in his image,
That you will die in disgrace in the sight of the barons,
Both you and all your people and all for your insult."

XXIV

"Beaumanoir," says Brambroc, "This is great folly,
That you put to death by your presumption
The flower of the duchy, by so very great a folly.
For when they are dead, and have passed from this life,
Nevermore will you find the like of them in this duchy."

"Brambroc," says Beaumanoir, "Don't you believe
That I have led here the noblest of the chivalry.
Laval, Rochefort, Lohéac are not here.
Nor are Montfort, Rohan, Quentin, a whole grand company.
But I have here certain noble knights
And the flower of the squires of all Brittany,

Who do not deign to flee, neither from life nor death.

Nor will they commit treason, falsity, or perfidy.

Each has sworn to God, to the Son of Holy Mary

That you will die in disgrace in the sight of the company,

And you and all of yours, whatever you may say,

Will be taken and tied up before the hour of Compline."

And Brambroc replied, "I take all your power and lordship

As less than a bud of garlic. For despite you, this day

I will have the mastery, and will conquer all Brittany and Normandy."

XXV

Brambroc says to the English, "My lords, the Bretons are wrong.

Lay on, strike, put them all to death, make sure

That none escapes me, neither weak nor strong."

All sixty were ready to attack.

At the first clash the discouragement was great.

Charruel was taken, Geffroi Moelon was killed

And the valiant Tristan, who was tall and strong

Was struck by the hammer to his pain and injury

Sir Jehan Rousselot was struck and nearly killed.

If Jesus Christ should not take notice,

Who takes all to safe harbor,

The Bretons would be overcome, I am sure.

XXVI

Great was the battle in the grassy meadow,

Caro de Bodegat was crushed by the hammer

And the valiant Tristan was mortally struck.

Then he exclaimed very loudly "Beaumanoir, where are you?

The English drive me so, wounded and smashed.

I have never been afraid any day when I could see you.

If the true God does not take notice, by His holy virtue
The English will lead me away
And you will have lost me."
Beaumanoir swears by God who was hung on the Cross,
That before that would be, many a rough blow would be struck,
Many a lance broken, and many a shield pierced.
At these words he draws his good sharp sword
Those who take a blow from it are dead or knocked down.
The English vigorously defend themselves from him.
They all think his power is but a bundle of straw.

XXVII

The battle was hard and the slaughter was cruel,
And on both sides they have the hearts of lions.
And all made a petition and agreement
To go all to seek a drink without delay.
Each one had a bottle of good wine of Anjou.
When all had drunk by agreement,
They returned to battle without any delay.

XXVIII

Great was the battle in the middle of the field,
And horrible was the slaughter, and hard was the tumult.
The Bretons have the worst of it, I cannot lie.
For two of them are dead and have passed from this life,
And three are prisoners, God come to their aid!
There remain only twenty-five in the battle.
But Geffroi de la Roche, a most noble squire
Of great lineage, asked for knighthood.
And Beaumanoir gave it to him in the name of Holy Mary,
And says to him, "Good sweet son, don't spare yourself now.

Remember those who for chivalry were at Constantinople

In good company." And Geffroi swore by God,

Who has all in his disposition, that the English would pay dear

In the hour of Compline.

And Brambroc hears it, and values their power,

And grand seigneurie at less than a bud of garlic.

Rather, he says to Beaumanoir with much great presumption,

"Surrender quickly, Beaumanoir, I will not kill you

But I will make of you a present to my lady love.

For I have promised to her and I do not lie to her,

That today I will lead you into her pleasure chamber."

And Beaumanoir replies, "I'll do you one better.

We hear you well, me and my company.

If it please the King of Glory, and Saint Mary,

And the good St. Yves in whom I have great faith,

Throw the dice, and don't hold back

The luck will fall on you, your life will be short."

XXIX

Alain de Keranrais also heard it and said to him,

"Brigand traitor, what are you thinking?

You think you will silence a man of such courage?

With my own body, I defy you today

On his behalf. Now I will strike you with my sharp lance!"

That moment, in everybody's view,

Alain de Keranrais struck him with his sharp steel lance

In the middle of the face, and his point has pierced him

To the brain. He extended his lance so that Brambroc has fallen.

Brambroc leapt to his feet and thought to engage him.

Sir Geffroi du Bois saw his position and also

Struck him with a lance so Brambroc fell dead,

Knocked to the earth.

Then du Bois cried out, "Beaumanoir, where are you?

By this you are avenged, he lies stretched out dead."

And Beaumanoir replied, for he had heard it well,

"My lords, fight strongly, the time is come!

God, go to the others, leave this one behind."

XXX

Now the English indeed saw that Brambroc was dead

And their pride and great audacity fell.

Then Croquart, a mad German, called out,

"You should know in truth that Brambroc who leads us

Has failed us.

All the books of Merlin which he loved so much

Were not worth two pennies. He lies, mouth gaping,

Dead and overthrown. I pray you, my good lords,

Act like prudent men, hold yourselves tightly together,

Those who come against you should be dead or maimed."

God! How much Beaumanoir will be distressed if those are not

abandoned to shame and contempt!

At these words, Charruel is on his feet, and the valiant Tristan,

Who was so badly wounded, and Caro de Bodegat

The preux and the honored. All three were prisoners of

Brambroc the mad,

But when Brambroc was dead they were freed.

Each one took in his hands the good sharp swords.

They have a good will to strike the English.

XXXI

After the death of Brambroc, that bold warrior,

The battle was great and the combat was heavy,

And the slaughter was horrible and wonderful and great.

There remained Master Croquart the German,

And Thomelin Belifort who looked like a giant,

Who fought with a heavy hammer of steel

And Hugh de Calveley was as much a part of it,

And Sir Robert Knolles, who was evil and crafty

And all their companions, and all the rest

Germans and Englishmen, in consternation they go and say,

"Let us avenge Brambroc our loyal friend, put them all to death,

Spare none of them, the day will be ours

Before the sun sets."

But Beaumanoir the noble came right up to them,

He and his companions whom he loved so well.

There commenced a slaughter very cruel and very woeful,

And the great blows which they struck each other on the head

Resounded a quarter league around.

There died two Englishmen and one good German,

And D'Ardaine the turncoat mercenary

Was dead and fallen on the green field.

Also Geffroi Poulart who stretched out

In the deepest of sleeps.

And Beaumanoir the bold warrior was wounded.

And if Jesus Christ, the Almighty Father,

Does not concern himself with it,

Neither side will come through it.

XXXII

Great was the battle and it lasted long,

And the slaughter was horrible on this side and that

This was on a Saturday when the sun rose

In the year Thirteen Hundred Fifty, believe me who will,

Before the Sunday when Holy Church sings

Laetare Jerusalem. In this holy time

They fought each other powerfully,

Nor did they spare each other.

The heat was great, each one was covered with sweat,

The ground was bedewed with sweat and blood.

That day Beaumanoir was fasting,

And the baron had great thirst, and asked for a drink.

Sir Geffroi du Bois straightaway replied,

"Drink your blood, Beaumanoir, your thirst will pass!

Today we have the honor, each one will gain

Such valiant renown that he indeed will never be reproached!"

Beaumanoir the valiant then strove his best,

Such grief he had and such anger that his thirst passed.

And on either side the slaughter began,

They were killed and wounded, hardly any escaped.

XXXIII

Terrible was the battle and the slaughter was mortal,

Halfway between Josselin and Ploërmel

In a meadow so very beautiful, by a little stream

At the place called the Halfway Oak,

A long, green and beautiful field covered with broom.

There were all the English gathered together in a phalanx,

Calveley the valiant, that bold youth,

And Thomas Belifort who fought with a hammer,

Anyone hit with it on the nape of his neck

Will nevermore eat either bread or cake.

Beaumanoir looks at them, they were not a pretty sight.

He saw the little game had become a great grief.

He was profoundly discouraged, now assist him St. Michael!

Sir Geffroi du Bois, who was strong and ready

Comforted him nobly as a young gentleman ought,

And says, "Gentle baron, see here Charruel,

The good Tinténiac, and Robin Raguenel,

Guillaume de la Marche and Olivier Arrel,

And Guy de Rochefort—see his pennoncel!

There is none of them but has lance, sword and dagger,

And all of them are here to fight like noble youths.

Again they will do new harm to the English."

XXXIV

Great was the battle, never have I heard of such a one.

The English held themselves tightly together,

No man came upon them without death or wounding,

All are in a phalanx, as though tied together.

Guillaume Montauban, the preux and well-honored

Came back from the fight and looked at them intently.

Great determination took him, his heart is swollen

And he swears by Jesus Christ Who hung on the Cross

That if he was mounted on a good horse, as he would like

He would break them up, to their shame and contempt.

Then he put great sharp spurs on his feet,

He mounted a great spirited horse,

And then took a lance with a squared steel point.

This prudent squire appeared to be fleeing.

Beaumanoir looked at him, then harangued him

And says, "Friend Guillaume, what are you thinking?

Would you leave like a false and evil squire?

You and your heirs to come will be reproached."

When Guillaume heard this, he smiles

And speaks in a loud voice, easily heard.

"Do what you must, Beaumanoir, noble and prudent knight,

For I will do what needs to be done. This is all I intend!"

Then he spurred the horse's flanks

So that the blood so red fell on the field.

He cast himself against the English,

And seven of them he has overthrown,

And coming back he has beat down three more.

This blow scattered the English, they all lost heart,

In very truth.

Whoever wishes has his choice of them, taking them

And receiving their parole.

Montauban shouts when he sees this,

"Montjoie" he cries, "Barons, strike now!

Try your hand, all of you, noble and prudent knights,

Tinténiac the good, preux and highly honored,

And Guy de Rochefort, Charruel the Gloomy,

And all of us companions whom God has benefited,

Avenge yourselves on the English at your will!"

XXXV

Great was the battle, and the combat was finished,

Tinténiac the good was the first in praise

Among Beaumanoir's men. Because of this deed,

One always hears people speak of him.

The English had lost their strength and their power,

One is pledged, another is a prisoner,

Knolles and Calveley are in great danger,

And Thomas Belifort has nothing left but his anger.

And all their companions, without any delay,

On account of the strong and fierce Brambroc's emprise,

Were led away to Castle Josselin — Sir Jean Plesanton,

Raoul the warrior, Helecoq his brother,

Whom one should not forget,

The valiant Repefort and de la Lande the fierce.

And you often hear this battle spoken about,

For it is one that old people should talk about,

And everyone should make romances about it,

One in written accounts, and another painting tapestries,

In all the realms near the sea,

If one wishes to astound many a noble knight,

Or many a noble lady of famous beauty

Just as one speaks about Arthur and Charlemagne

Guillaume of the Short Nose, and Roland and Olivier.

Concerning this battle of the Thirty, which was without peer,

People will romance three hundred years from now.

XXXVI

Great was the battle, there is no doubt of that,

The English defeated, who out of envy wished

To have power and lordship over the Bretons.

So pray to God who was born of Mary,

For all those who were in that company,

Bretons or English.

Pray to God that none shall be damned on Judgment Day,

That St. Michael and St. George should help them that day,

Say now to all of them, "Amen,"

For all that God has given to them.

Two views of the Siege of Calais (4 September 1346–3 August 1347). The English capture and control of the port of Calais provided a foothold to launch their invasions into the French interior throughout the Hundred Years War; and the French would not recapture the city until 1558. These two images show how later artists would re-imagine a battle to suit their own artistic interests, often independent of actual events. Although there were early attempts to scale the walls, repeated attempts to lift the siege by sea, and King Philip of France would eventually put an army into the field, there was neither a field battle, nor a sortie beyond the walls: as with most sieges, the city ultimately fell due to deprivation and disease.

Above: From Jean Froissart, *Chroniques*. Paris, Virgil Master (illuminator); c. 1410. The Hauge, KB 72 A 25, 162v. Below: Mid-15th century, Bibliothèque Nationnale de France.

Battle between the French and the English on the coast of Brittany. The two sides carry their standards, one blue with the golden lilies of France, the other red with the English leopard.

From Jean Froissart, *Chronicles*; c. 1410. MS 864, folio 91, Bibliotheque Municipale, Besancon, France.

Their sweeping defeat at Crécy in 1346 by a vastly smaller army had left French chivalry anxious to prove their mettle and prowess at arms—in battle, skirmish or deed of arms—setting the stage for encounters like the Combat of the Thirty, which was all three of these things in equal measure.

From Jean Froissart, *Chroniques* (Vol. I),c. 1410. British Library, Cotton Nero E. II pt.2, f.152v.

Only a year after the humiliating defeat at Crécy, France and her Breton allies suffered another set-back when Charles de Blois, the French claimaint to the dukedom of Brittany, was captured in battle by Thomas Dagworth. Charles would spend the next nine years in prison before his massive ransom could be raised, but the War of Succession would continue on in his name.

From Jean Froissart, *Chroniques*; c. 1410. The Hauge, KB 72 A 25, folio 155r.

Battle scene between soldiers in armor carrying lances. Although an early 15th-century (c. 1410) depiction of mid-14th-century events, the image accurately portrays the growing popularity and interest in deeds of arms fought on foot, whether in single or group combat, as opposed to the mounted melee.

From Jean Froisssart, *Chronicles*, Ms 865 f. 1, one of four vignettes on this page. Bibliotheque Municipale Besanon.

Another depiction of the Battle of Auray, this time showing the fighting as a close-quarters foot battle. These contradictory images of the same event are a good reminder that chronicles were often composed years after the original events from a combination of eye-witness and second-hand accounts, and even the most critical details could shift or blur in the process.

From Jean Froissart, *Chroniques*; c. 1410. The Hauge, KB 72 A 25, folio 257r.

taille de la taille il ont sens, /
toute que ce est la merueille
et le myreor de toutes les dames

eulx enfant. de celui len voit
len bien garder. na cbr en ceste
place tant fort. ne tant preuz

This image of knights engaged in a tournament while a queen and her entourage watch from a balcony was created only a year or so after the famous contest of the 30 English and 30 French. Although an Italian illustration, depicting a friendly deed of arms, it much more closely depicts the harness and equipment that would have been worn by the French knights in the Combat of the Thirty, than most chronicles of the actual event, which were recorded and a generation or more after the event.

Helie de Borron, *Le Roman du Roi Meliadus de Leonnoys*; 1352. Add 12228. Folio No: 214v–215, British Library.

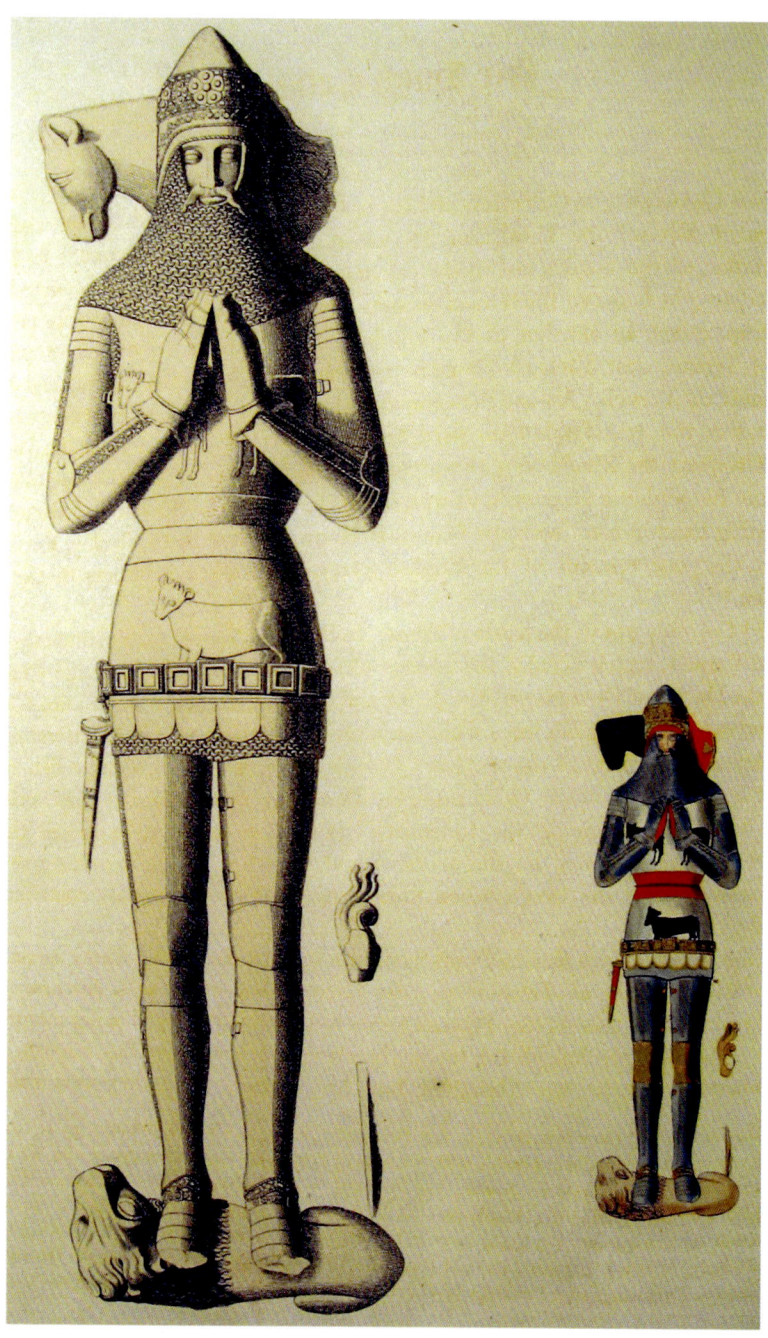

The effigy of Hugh Calveley (c. 1320s to 1394). Born the youngest son of David de Calveley of Lea, and his wife, Joanna, it is possible that he was a close relative, maybe even a half-brother, of Sir Robert Knolles, who also fought in the Combat of the Thirty. Calveley won his spurs, and his fame in the Breton War of Succession, and had command of the reserve division of the forces of Jean de Montfort, at the Battle of Auray. Calveley fared less well in the Thirty, being captured and held to ransom

Charles Alfred Stothard, *The Monumental Effigies of Great Britain* (1813), pg 98.

A rare example of a 14th-century haubergeon and aventail mounted on a cervellière. This armor would have provided a second line of defense for English men-at-arms or French knights, if their substantial plate armor was penetrated, but would have formed the principle harness for Franco-Breton squires or men-at-arms.

c.1340 German Haubergeon and Aventail, c. 1340, Royal Armouries, Leeds.

An early side-mount bascinet, such as would have been worn by both English and French knights at the Combat of Thirty.

Royal Armouries, Leeds (RA IV.497).

The cervellière was a small iron skull-cap, initially worn over a mail coif and under a great helm. Over the early decades of the 14th century, the coif was replaced with an aventail that attached directly to the cervellière, and the skull cap grew into the more complete, bascinet.

German Aventail and early bascinet or *cervellière*, c. 1340, Royal Armouries, Leeds.

A doublet attributed to Charles of Blois, and likely worn around the time of his death at the Battle of Auray. This doublet has an outer layer of patterned silk and a padded body, particularly throughout the chest, and was designed to give the wearer the silhouette of a broad chest and narrow, elongated waist. Although a civilian garment, it is believed that the padded pourpoints, or gambesons, worn by English and French knights and nobles would have followed a similar pattern.

Musee Historique des Tissus, Lyons, France.

Centuries after it was fought, the Combat of the Thirty, a militarily and politically insignificant event, has continued to inspire artists, as seen in this 19th- century depiction of the waning moments of the battle.

Octave Penguilly-L'Haridon, *Les Combat des Trente* (1857), Musee des Beau-Arts de Quimper.

Jehan de Beaumanoir continues to be remembered in his native Brittany, as attested to by this modern bronze statue of the knight bearing a sword and shield blazoned with his coat of arms which stands in the heart of Dinan, ducal seat of the old duchy.

Arthur Guéniot (1866–1951) sculptor, inaugurated 16 July 1911.

4.

Androw of Wyntoun's Account

Of a battle that took place then between the French and the English.

> In this time of which I tell
> An adventure in France befell
> That for the doughtiness of the deed
> Deserves to be both written and read.
> All that belongs to this matter
> I think it profitable to write here
> That men of arms may have rejoicing
> When they come to hear it.
> In Little Brittany beyond the sea
> There took place a war of fair battle
> Between French and Englishmen
> At the encounter there were more Englishmen
> Than were French, yet all their company

Was defeated completely in the fighting.

The lord of Beaumanoir in battle

Manfully approached an English knight

That spoke of Frenchmen quite lightly

And would often say scornfully

"What, are not the English the doughtiest men

Though God may sleep in his den?

Yet I think and I think it true

One Englishman is worth Frenchmen two."

Thus he often spoke until the day

This lord of Beaumanoir said to him

"You speak, sir, too freely

Men may perchance find near at hand

Men of such quality

As you may find in your country."

The knight said, "Sir, by my faith

That I would like to put to the test

Where we could fight with even sides.

And I would like to be one of them."

Beaumanoir then was angered

And said to him, "You may find perchance

Your fill of fighting if you dare."

"Yes, God willing," said he, "I will be there."

"Good sir," says Beaumanoir, "perhaps

If you wish to put it to the test

I shall make the covenant.

You shall go home to England

And choose of the best men in your country

Until there be thirty-one

And I shall choose as many for myself

Of kin and friends here with me

And let us set here a certain place

To meet, and if God gives me grace

I will have victory with my retinue.

If you shall be slain in the combat

Your ransom I will forgive you.

I shall not ask for anything

And if you are taken to prison

Then shall you double your ransom to me.

So shall men see if French can deal

As fiercely with Englishmen.

Oh, mighty God of Heaven!" he said,

"How your worship and your prowess

Should be increased manifold

If you will to your covenant hold."

"This," said he, "I shall certainly do."

Their covenant they made in haste,

And set for them a certain place,

By Caen in Normandy.

When they had arranged the day

This knight to England went away

And openly told these tidings,

And the word sped through the land

That, except for war, this was such a good thing,

That young men who yearned to win praise

Would proffer service to their lords

So that they might leave

And secure that they might

In the number of that thirty fight.

Then in the English sea went he

To chose there of gentle birth

Thirty, all their boldest men.

That he could choose in England then;

And Beaumanoir went into his land

And of his friends that were near at hand

And of his kin chose thirty

Bold and skillful, strong and doughty,

And privily he made inquiry

Of all the men that with him were

Who loved *par amours* and where they loved.

And where he heard there lovers were,

He made sure so subtly

That if a maiden were his lady

That he so loved, then he secured

That she should be at the fighting;

And if she were bound in wedlock

Her lord should bring her thither with him.

For where such things were a-do

He thought it was fit

That the sight of fair ladies

Should take away any thought of cowardice.

Thus he brought all their ladies there

So they should fight in their sight, but more,

For he supposed that being in their sight

Should give them hardihood and might.

The day came soon, and in the place

A stalwart barrier was made there

Of great ropes of bast pierced

Through posts that right deep were dug.

Within the earth right stalwartly

And thither came of each party

Thirty on each side to fight.

The Frenchmen were gaily adorned

With horses covered in iron and steel,

But the Englishmen had no

Armored horse, as I heard say

For they as soon as they had come

To their end of the lists, they lit down

And made them ready to fight on foot.

The Frenchmen just so have done

Seeing them dismount they got down soon

And together they met with spears straight

And a long while they thrust and fought.

One Englishman had upon a staff

A hammer head, and with it gave such blows

That at their clashing

He slew one beyond recovering.

So fast their force they put to the test

That both the parties lost their wind.

A little they withdrew then

And on their swords did lean

But then one of the French squires

Saw by the fight, and their array

That victory would be hard to win

Without subtlety or stratagem.

He left his comrades where they stood

And even toward his horse he went

The lord of Beaumanoir who saw

Him, as he thought, withdraw

Said, "Cousin, I never guessed of ye

That you be the first to give way."

He said, "The ram often retreats

That he may continue the fight."

This answer he made briefly

And continued on to his horse in haste
Leaped on, and again galloping he came
And found them fast fighting.
At the side of the Englishmen
So stoutly he drove in
That he rudely scattered them.
And where he saw the greatest assembly
Of Englishmen, there he rode.
And roughly made room among them
For his horse was well armed
So that he dreaded stabbing the less.
The Frenchmen saw them scattered,
Rushed on them, without dread or fear
And defeated them utterly.
Nine were slain of their company,
And the rest were all taken.
Of Frenchmen there died none
Apart from him who with the maul
Was slain, as you heard before.
The Frenchmen were valued highly
Because when they in such haste
Saw their fellow withdraw
As if it had been in dread and fear
They made no sign of dismay
For his sudden withdrawing
But fought on fiercely as before
And did not hesitate nevertheless.
That was to be praised, and so was he
That in so fierce a hot affray
As man for man and outnumbered
As they were, they with wit could deal,

And for the manner through which they won
This battle that was fought then
And ended where ladies gallant
Might see right well how manfully
Their lovers bore themselves in that fight,
And I trust they would when they might
Reward them privately
With solace and ease for their prowess.
Now by understanding this fight
Men may see arrogant pride and hauteur
Caused this fight to be undertaken.
Further men may see that it makes no sense
To despise other nations,
For men may well see, by reason,
That they are men as much as they are,
And will perchance prove as good
As they are, further should none despise
Their foes, for the victory lies
In their valour as well as his own.
Therefore I think that he is wrong who thinks
That another man little or nothing is worth,
Who bears him better when he comes forth.

Appendix 1

The Combatants and Their Arms

It is impossible to be certain about who took part in the Combat of Thirty against Thirty. In fact, the sources leave it unclear whether each side consisted of thirty in addition to or including its captain. A variety of lists were compiled by early Breton authors. The safest source would seem to be the anonymous poet, who wrote only a very few years after the event, and claimed to know every name. His testimony does not settle the matter, because the two manuscripts of his poem give somewhat different lists. Further, many of the names have been garbled, especially the English ones. My list and my short comments on the careers of the participants, where known, follow H. R. Brush's introduction to his edition of the poem; Brush derived some of his information from De Courcy's 1857 book on the Combat, which I have not seen. More details on the Combatants and how they have been identified can be found in those two works. Some of the Bretons I have marked as "otherwise unknown" were nevertheless members of known families. I have not bothered to mark unknown Englishmen this way, since most of them are entirely unidentifiable.

In his edition and translation of the poem in 1827, G.A. Crapelet presented a list of the Breton Combatants. His roll of honor differs from Brush's by including thirty-one rather than thirty individuals, ten knights and twenty-one squires.

Crapelet was certain he could identify the heraldic devices of all but two of them. Even though Crapelet's list is probably less reliable than that produced by Brush, I have included it with blazons of the attributed arms in the belief that many readers will be interested.

The Bretons

1. **Jean de Beaumanoir**. He was a prominent knight of Brittany whose career is known from both chronicles and archival records.

2. **The Lord of Tinténiac**. He held fiefs in both Brittany and Normandy. He was killed in battle in 1352 at Mauron.

3. **Guy de Rochefort**, Lord of Harleix, militarily active in the 1350s.

4. **Yves (Yvain) Charruel, Lord of Guérand**. A prominent warrior whose career stretched from about 1342 to 1369.

5. **Robin Raguenel**, Lord of Châteauloger. Son of a prominent counselor of early fourteenth-century dukes, was himself the father of Tiphaine, first wife of Bertrand du Guesclin.

6. **Caro de Bodégat**. Known only as an associate of Gui de Rochefort and Huet Catus.

7. **Guillaume de la Marche**. A knight, killed at Mauron with Tinténiac.

8. **Olivier Arrel, Lord of Kermarquer**. Fought at La Roche Derrien in 1347.

9. **Jehan Rousselet**. Nephew of a bishop, Raoul of St. Malo and Laon.

10. **Geffroi du Bois**. There were many Breton families named "du Bois."

11. **Guillaume de Montauban**. He rode the horse to finish the Combat, and also fought at Mauron.

12. **Alain de Tinténiac**. His military career began as early as 1344 and extended at least to 1356.

13. **Tristan de Pestivien**. Younger brother of the baron of that name.

14. **Alain de Keranrais.** Otherwise unknown.

15. **Olivier de Keranrais.** Uncle of Alain.

16. **Louys Gouyon (Goyon or Gouëon).** A younger son of the Lord of Matignon

17. **Olivier de Fontenoy.** A companion of Du Bois, Pestivien, Keranrais, and Gouyon. There is some uncertainty about whether there was a second Fontenoy in the Combat.

18. **Huet (Hauguet or Hugues) Catus, Lord of Breuil in Poitou.** An associate of Rochefort and Bodégat.

19. **Geffroi de la Roche.** Otherwise unknown.

20. **Geffroi Poulart.** His family was associated with the Blois dynasty.

21. **Morice de Trézéguidy.** He had a long career, and was still alive in 1395. Christine de Pisan mentioned him in a letter as an example of loyalty comparable to Du Guesclin.

22. **Guyon de Pont Blanc.** Otherwise unknown.

23. **Morice du Parc.** He had a prominent military career in later life.

24. **Geffroi de Beaucors (Beaucorps).** Otherwise unknown.

25. **(Geslin) Lanlop or Villong.** Lanlop seems to have been his surname or chief fief, with Villong being another one he held.

26. **Geffroi Moelon (Mellon).** Otherwise unknown.

27. **Jehannot de Serrant (Desserain).** Son of the Lord of Tromeur.

28. **Olivier Monteville**. Otherwise unknown.

29. **Guillaume de la Lande.** A younger son of a family based at Guichen.

30. **Simon Richard (Pachart?), Lord of Kerjean.** His public career lasted until the 1380s.

The English

1. **Robert Brambroc, Bamborough, Brandenburg, Brandebourch.** The name of the English leader shows up in a variety of forms, but no one knows anything definite about him, including whether he himself was German. It is suggestive that there is a place named Bamborough in Cheshire, the source of many English warriors in this era. (Brush for some reason calls him "Richard.")

2. **Robert Knolles.** From Cheshire, originally of "base extraction," but afterwards an extraordinarily successful captain.

3. **Hugh Calveley (Calverley).** Another Cheshireman, whose career flourished after his participation in the Combat.

4. **Croquart.** A Dutch or German mercenary, rose from the lowly position of page or valet, he died in a fall from a fast horse not long after the Combat.

5. **Plesanton.**

6. **Ridele.**

7. **Helecoq.**

8. **Repefort.**

9. **Jannequin Taillart.**

10. **Richard de la Lande "Le Fier" (the fierce).** Still active in the 1370s.

11. **Thomelin (Thomas) Belifort.**

12. **Hueceton Clamaban (Clomean).**

13. **Renequin Hérouart.** This may be the old English name "Hereward."

14. **Hulbure (Huebnie).** Was Hulbure "old" or was this the "villein" that the poet accuses the English captain of introducing into his team? Different readings in the two manuscripts make it impossible to be sure.

15. **Jannequin Betonchamp (Begurcamp).**

16. **Gaule l'Alemant.** His name indicates that he was German.

17. **Jeannequin (Rennequin) Mareschal.**

18. **Thomelin Houlnanton (Houalton)**

19. **Robinet Melipart**

20. **Helichon (Harclou) "le Musart" (the fool)**

21. **Isinnay (Isanay).** Took part in the attempted relief of Bécherel in 1363.

22. **Bicquillay.**

23. **Troussel.** A man called Troussel fought Du Guesclin at Rennes in 1356.

24. **Robin Adés.** Fighting under Knolles he captured Du Guesclin in 1352.

25. **Huelton le Contart (Dango the Fleet).** Identity uncertain. He may have been a James d'Andelé who fought with Knolles, in 1356.

26. **Nicholas (John) Dagworth.** Nephew of the Thomas Dagworth (called "Dagorne" by the poet) who was the English lieutenant in Brittany until shortly before the Combat. Brush identifies the nephew as the Nicholas Dagworth whose spectacular funeral brass survives at Blickling in Norfolk. Sumption, however, believes the Combatant in question was named John Dagworth.

27. **Perrot de Commellan.** He was a member of a known Breton family.

28. **Guillemin (Hamon) le Gaillart.** Another member of a known Breton family.

29. **Raoulet d'Aspremont.** A Breton known from other records.

30. **D'Ardaine.** A member of a baronial Breton family.

Crapelet's List of the Bretons and Their Arms

Knights

1.   **Robert (sic) de Beaumanoir.** Azure, eleven billets argent, 4, 3, and 4.

2.   **The Lord of Tinténiac.** Ermine, a crescent gules.

3.   **Guy de Rochefort.** Counter-vairy or and azure.

4.   **Yves Charruel.** Gules, a fess argent.

5.   **Robin Raguenel.** Quarterly argent and sable, a label counterchanged in chief.

6.   **Huon de Saint-Yvon.** Argent, a cross sable, a bendlet gules overall.

7.   **Caro de Bodegat.** Gules, three bezants ermine.

8.   **Olivier Arrel.** Quarterly argent and azure.

9.   **Geoffrey du Bois.** Of all the possibilities, Crapelet chose Azure, three swords inverted in fess argent.

10. **Jean Rousselot.** Argent, three battle-axes sable.

Squires

1.   **Guillaume de Montauban.** Gules, nine mascles or, a label of 4 argent.

2.   **Alain de Tinténiac.** As in 2 above, Ermine, a crescent gules.

3.   **Tristan de Pestivien.** Vairy argent and sable.

4.   **Alain de Keranrais.** Vairy argent and gules.

5.   **Olivier de Keranrais, his uncle.** Vairy argent and gules (Same as Alain de Keranrais).

6.   **Louis Goyon.** Argent, a lion gules crowned or.

7.   **Geoffroy de la Roche.** Gules, three lanceheads or, 2 and 1.

8.   **Guyon de Pontblanc.** Or, ten billets sable 4, 3, 2, and 1.

9.   **Geoffroy de Beaucorps ou de Beaucors.** No arms found.

10.   **Maurice du Parc.** Argent, three bars gemels gules.

11.   **Jean de Serent.** Or, three cinquefoils sable.

12.   **N. de Fontenay.** Argent, three bendlets gemels gules.

13.   **Hugues Capus, Chapus, or Trapus.** No arms found.

14.   **Geoffroy Poulard.** Quarterly, 1st and 4th gules, a rose argent seeded or, 2nd and 3rd vert.

15.   **N. Tréziguidy #1.** Or, three pine cones gules 2 and 1.

16.   **N. Tréziguidy #2.** Or, three pine cones gules 2 and 1 (Same as N. Tréziguidy #1).

17.   **Guillaume de la Lande.** Gules, a fess counter-embattled argent.

18.   **Olivier de Monteville.** Barry argent and gules of ten, a bordure sable.

19.   **Simon Richard.** Azure, a stag's massacre or, and in chief a rose argent between two plates.

20.   **Geoffroy de Mellon or Meslon.** Azure, three crosses patté argent.

21.   **Guillaume de la Marche.** Gules, a chief argent.

Appendix 2

Armor of the Combat of the Thirty, 1351

by Douglas Strong

When analyzing the armor worn at the Combat of the Thirty we find ourselves making some assumptions and generalizations, given the limited data available. Foremost among these is an understanding that there is a difference in the way the combatants were armed. This differentiation was based on national origin or allegiance and on social standing or wealth. Clearly those knights who were more wealthy and powerful, such as the commanders of each force, would have been better outfitted than the knights, esquires, and men-at-arms who served under their command.

When looking at the question of national influences, things become more challenging. The combatants were of English and Breton origin. The Bretons were divided in their allegiance and represented warriors on both sides of the combat. This complicates matters quite a great deal. There is precious little information about Breton armor in the 14th century, while there is quite a bit of information about English and French armor and they are actually quite distinct and different. While we can say with some certainty how English knights would have been equipped, the Bretons present more of a challenge. Were some armored in the French manner because of their French allegiance and others armored in the English manner because of their English allegiance? Were all the Bretons—regardless of allegiance—armored in the manner of Frenchmen because of their geographic connection to mainland France? Was there a unique Breton style of arming of which we are unaware? This is impossible to tell. Herein I will make the assumption that the allegiance of the Breton forces influenced the way in which they equipped themselves. I will describe the Breton forces under Sir Jean de Beaumanoir as being armed in the French manner and the English forces under Sir Robert Brandebourch as being armed according to their own, native, fashion.

In addition to acknowledging some of the assumptions and generalizations being made, it is important that we acknowledge the impact of the time in which this battle took place. The combat occurred right in the middle of the greatest change in the development of armor, a period frequently referred to as the "transitional period," where knights switched from mail as their primary form of defense to rigid plate armor. Due to this, there may have been a great deal of variation in the combatants' armor that goes beyond national allegiance or social status. This was an age of experimentation, and variation was the norm rather than the exception.

With regards to to the sources of the information upon which these discussions are based, I primarily drew from two main sources. First, I have statistically analyzed over 1300 monumental effigies and memorial brasses between 1300 and 1450.[1] It is upon this analysis that I have based my discussion of what was typical for the time period. When dealing with effigies and brasses it is important to remember that these were often created after (sometimes long after) the deaths of the person who is represented in the effigy. They frequently represent fashions for clothing and armor at the time of the memorial's creation rather than at any particular point in the life of the owner. This is most evident in the effigy of the Combat of the Thirty participant, Sir Hugh Calveley.[2] This effigy

---

[1]   http://talbotsfineaccessories.com/armour/effigy/effigy%20analysis.html
[2]   http://www.bunbury.org.uk/papers/Sir_Hugh_frameset.html

was created about the time of his death nearly half a century after the combat in question. Its armor perfectly represents a wealthy knight in the middle of the 1390s, and it would be a grave mistake to assume this was how Sir Hugh arrayed himself for the Combat in 1351. The second source of information for this article is my examination of the small group of surviving armors from the period of the Combat. These pieces provide us with the minute details needed to understand what we are seeing in the effigies and brasses.

One final acknowledgement of methodology would be valuable here. When describing the difference between those of higher social status (the knights) and those of lower status (the squires and men-at-arms), I have relied on the fact that the Combat of the Thirty took place on the cusp of two decades. When describing the array of the knights I have relied on examples from the 1350s and when describing the squires and men-at-arms I have drawn from equipment of the 1340s. While by no means foolproof, it does present a logical division, and presents the reader with some of the diversity that would have been present on the fields of Mars at this point in history.

The English Knights

English knights such as Sir Robert Brande-bourch would have probably been equipped in a distinctly English manner. The best armed English knights of this combat would have certainly worn a fully formed bascinet with an attached mail aventail to defend their heads and necks. These may have been worn with or without an attached visor. The visor would have been secured to the bascinet with side pivots and would probably have had a rounded or bluntly conical profile. These bascinets may have been supplemented by a great helm as well.

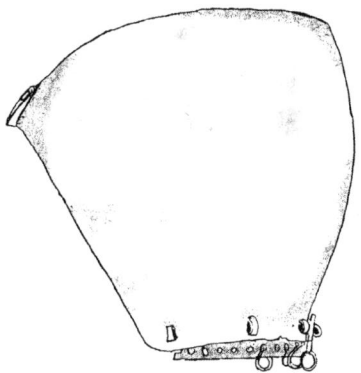

An early bascinet. Note the vervelles, or attachment points for the aventail, but the sill relatively close, bulbous and rounded shape of the CERVELLIÈRE.

The so-called "pig-faced bascinet," so closely associated with the 14th century, with its
sharply conical visor would not have made
an appearance on the field at this early date.
The torsos of the English knights would
have almost certainly been defended with
multiple layers of protection. The challenge
lies in interpreting what these layers might
have been due to the presence of the surcoat which covered the entire torso, thereby
hiding the layers beneath. At the inner-
most layer the knight would have worn a
durable and padded garment, often called
an aketon or gambeson, to absorb shock
and to keep his next layer from chafing.
The second layer would have been a full
coat of well-tailored, closely fitting mail.
While not as long as the hauberk of early
generations, this was still a relatively long
garment, falling onto the thighs. The next
layer is the problematic one. The mail and
occasionally the padding are frequently
visible on monumental effigies along the
lower edge of the surcoat, though any rigid
body defenses are almost always covered
by it. There is sometimes evidence of rigid
defenses in the form of a boss for a guard

*Despite having been seen as a "cultural
backwater" by continentals, military
fashion and technology amongst the
bellicose English had outpaced that of
France, as can be seen in this effigy of
William de Aldeburgh (d. 1358), who has
substantial plate defenses at all points
of his body.*

chain, either visible through, or seemingly attached to, the surcoat. Addition-
ally, many English effigies of this period have a somewhat rounded torso profile
suggestive of the globose breastplate which would become popular in later
years of the 14th century. Well over half of the effigies sampled show rounded

profiles to the torso. This strongly suggests a rigid body defense worn beneath the surcoat, which was either a globose cuirass or a coat of plates joined in a manner to create a rounded form such as can be seen on the misericord of the fallen rider in Lincoln Cathedral.[3]

The surcoat itself was going through stylistic changes of its own. The so-called "cyclas"—a style popular among English knights in the 1340s—was fading from use. In its place, a tight, side-laced surcoat with a relatively short but full skirt was making its debut.

The arms of the English knights would have been quite well defended. Their arms would have been fully encased in rigid plate arm harnesses. These would have been an even mix of fully articulated harnesses with each plate joined to the next with rivets for movement. Those whose plates were not articulated one to another would have been no less encompassing but they would have been joined one to another either through internal leather straps or by means of lacing points. Their hands would have been defensed with full gauntlets made of small plates in the manner of a coat of plates; several complete or nearly complete gauntlets of this type were found at the site of the Battle of Wisby which was fought on the island of Gotland in 1361. The most wealthy of these knights may have even begun to wear the hourglass gauntlets closely associated with the 14th century. These begin to appear in English effigies and brasses in the 1350s.

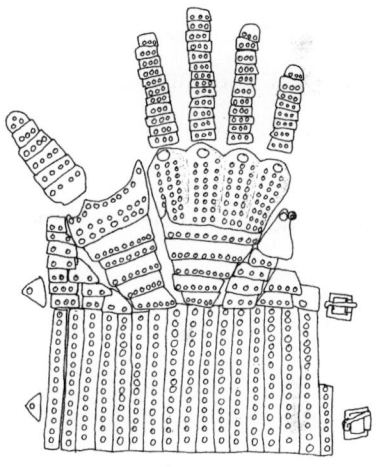

An early form of articulated, plate gauntlet, from the Battle of Wisby, 1361. By the time of Wisby, this style of gauntlet had largely been supplanted by the "hourglass" style, but in 1351, they would have predominated in the field.

---

3   David Edge and John Miles Paddock, *Arms and Armour of the Medieval Knight.* (New York: Crescent, 1988) 82.

The legs of the English knights would also have been well defended. Like the arm defenses, legs were completely encased in rigid plate. However, unlike the arms there is no sign at this date of the use of articulation to join the plates together. Rather, like many of the arms they would have been joined either through internal leather straps or by means of lacing points. Their feet would have been encased in fully developed sabatons with pointed toes.

The Breton Knights

Because of their proximity to mainstream France, Breton knights such as Sir Jean de Beaumanoir would likely have been armed in the fashion of French knights. French armor at this time was significantly different from—and one might fairly say—behind English armor at this period.

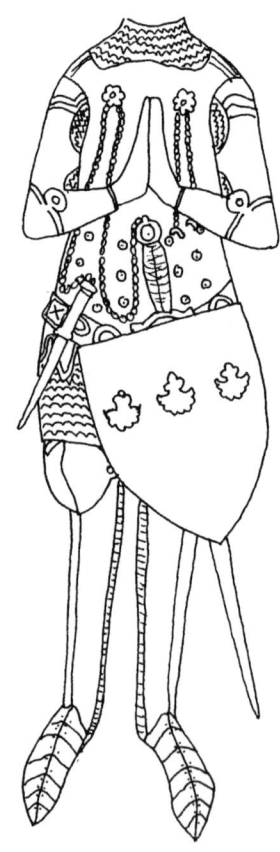

The best armed Breton knights of this combat would have certainly worn a bascinet of some form, but this would most likely not have had an attached aventail. French effigies of this period clearly show a predominance of mail coifs being worn, supplemented in some cases by separate bascinets. Bascinets without attached aventails rarely show any evidence of ever having visors attached to them. Therefore it is more likely that the Breton knights would have relied on great helms as either a supplement or replacement for the bascinet in order to provide some form of facial protection.

Like their English counterparts, the torsos of the Breton knights would have almost certainly been defended with multiple layers of protection. They also wore surcoats which covered their torsos, and undoubtedly also wore three layers of protection comprising a layer of padding, a layer of mail, and some form of rigid protection.

Pierre de Chantemelle, France

Unlike the English, the French fashion was for a more tubular torso and only about one third of the body armors have rounded chests. The remainder of the bodies were probably defended with simple coats of plates such as those found at Wisby.

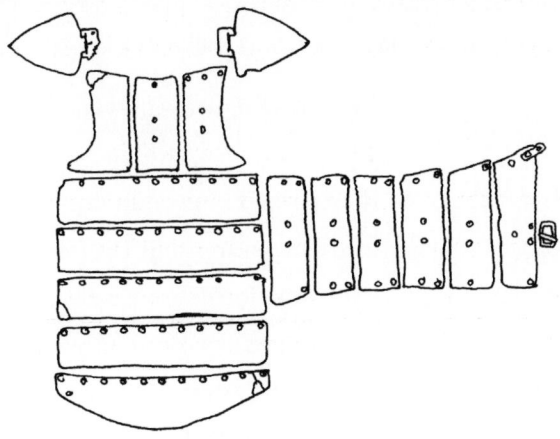

A surviving "coat of plates" body defense, found in the mass-burial pits from the Battle of Wisby, 1361. Although the wealthiest English knights might have worn a small, globose breastplate, the coat-of-plates would have been the most common plate defense for the torso found on the field at the Thirty.

The more fashionable of the Breton knights would have worn a shorter, tight surcoat similar to those worn by the Engish, but most of them likely wore looser surcoats which terminated between the knee and mid-thigh.

The arm defenses of Breton knights would have presented one of the most obvious differences between those armed in the English and French manners. More than half of the effigies of French knights surveyed in the 1350s still show their arms completely defended with mail sleeves. The remaining 45% had full floating arm harnesses joined by lacing points or internal leathers. At this period most French knights were still also using mail mittens as the primary hand defense.

The leg defenses worn by the Breton knights would have also differed from their English enemies. Fully defended legs joined without articulation would have probably been worn by about half of the knights while the remainder would probably have still been wearing mail chausses, occasionally supplemented with a knee plate or a greave plate. Their feet would have been similarly defended. Those with mail chausses would primarily have relied on the mail for their feet while those with full floating legs would probably have had full sabatons with pointed toes.

The English Squires and Men-at-Arms

Even with the advances in armor technology, complete plate defenses were still some decades away, and plate reinforcement was hardly in universal service, as can be seen in this effigy of Hugh Hastings (d. 1347). Although his arms arms are well-defended with plate armor and his surcoat is of the latest fashion, his visored bascinet is of an older, bulbous style, and he wears neither schynbalds nor sabatons to protect his lower legs and feet.

Like the English knights, the English squires and men-at-arms would have been better armed than their Breton counterparts. More than half of these squires and men-at-arms would have had some form of bascinet and many of them would have had attached aventails of mail. Like the knights, those with attached aventails may have had some form of visor attached. These combatants may also have relied on great helms for face protection when needed.

One can assume that the squires and men-at-arms bodies were defended like their knightly counterparts. English effigies of the 1340s show tubular torsos covered with surcoats. In about 10% of the cases there is evidence of the coat of plates extending below the front edge of the surcoat.

Arm harnesses would have shown a great deal of diversity. These arm defenses would have been of three types in roughly even numbers. The best-defended would have had full and fully articulated arm harnesses, while others would have had full arms joined with internal leathers or lacing. The last group would have had arms defended by mail, supplemented with a floating couters or forearm defense. More than half of the squires and men-at-arms would probably have had segmented gauntlets to defend their hands. The remaining group would have relied on mail mittens as hand protection.

All of the English squires and men-at-arms would have worn full chausses of mail as their leg protection, but over 70% of them would have supplemented this defense by adding floating poleyn and schynbalds (a plate shin defense) or greaves to protect their lower legs. Most would still have had mail as their primary protection for the feet but many would have added simple sabatons over this mail, which sometimes covered only the very tops of their feet and did not extend down to the ground as did those worn by knights. A sabaton of this sort was excavated at the battle of Wisby.[4]

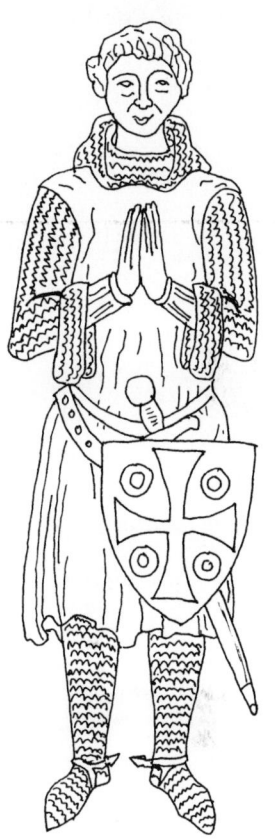

The Breton Squires

Breton squires and men-at-arms would have had the least advanced armor on the field at the Combat of the Thirty. Mail would have predominated as the main form of armor. Most of these combatants would have worn a mail coif into battle with a small hemispherical helmet, called a *cervellière*, without attached mail or a visor, relying on a great helm if greater protection was desired.

Like all of the other combatants, they would probably have had a coat of plates under their surcoat, but it is entirely possible that they did not, given the predominance of mail found on

As late as the mid-century, there were a number of French squires and men-at-arms entering battle relying on a defense comprised of nothing more than mail, a coat-of-plates and a shield—just as had their fathers and grandfathers before them.

---

4   Bengt Thordemann *Armour From the Battle of Wisby.* (Fig. 112).

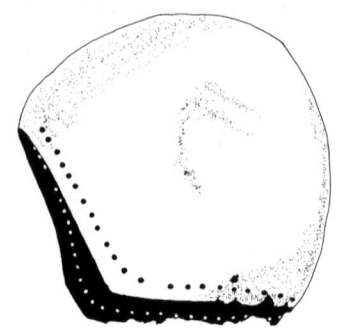

A CERVELLIÈRE, the small iron skull-cap, that was the forerunner to the bascinet.

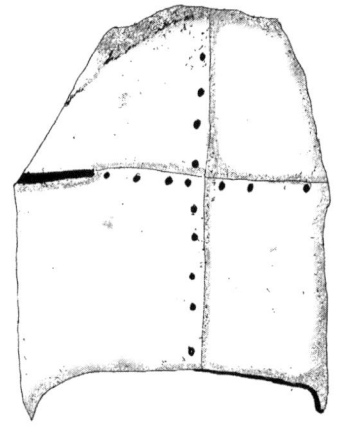

With the scarcity of fully developed and visored bascinets amongst the Breton forces, the older greathelm would still have seen use on the French side of the field, either worn alone, or more commonly, over the small CERVELLIÈRE.

other parts of their bodies as the primary form of defense. Only about 10% of French effigies from the 1340s show evidence of a coat of plates beneath the surcoat.

All of the Breton squires wore full sleeves of mail to protect their arms. About 10% of these soldiers would have added some form of rigid lower arm defense along with a circular roundel laced at the bend of the elbow. Most would have used mail mittens as their hand protection but about 15% of these would have been replaced with segmented gauntlets.

As was the case with arm defenses, all of the Breton squires would have worn mail chausses as their primary leg protection. However about a third of these soldiers would have added schynbalds, and some-times a poleyn for the knee. When shyn-balds were used soldiers occasionally added rudimentary sabatons but most relied on the mail feet attached to their chausses.

Conclusion

If our knowledge of armor from this period and the assumptions and gen-eralizations I have made about how the combatants were armed is accurate, we can see that not all the warriors came to the Combat of the Thirty equally equipped. The best armored of the English forces were much better defended than the best of the Breton forces. In fact the English squires and men-at-arms were nearly as well armored as the Breton knights. This left the Breton squires who depended primarily on mail in a distant fourth place in terms of quality of armor. Nevertheless, despite the differences in the quality of the armor, it was the Breton forces who prevailed.

Bibliography

Blair, Claude. *The Effigy and Tomb of Sir Hugh Caveley.*
http://www.bunbury.org.uk/papers/Sir_Hugh_frameset.html

Edge, David and John Miles Paddock, *Arms and Armour of the Medieval Knight.*
New York, Crescent, 1988.

Strong, Douglas W. *An Analysis of over 1300 Effigies Dated Between 1300 and 1450* http://talbotsfineaccessories.com/armour/effigy/effigy%20analysis.html

Thordemann, Bengt. *Armour from the Battle of Wisby.* 2 Vols. Stockholm, Sweden: 1939.

Bibliography

Editions and Translations

Ainsworth, William Harrison. "The Combat of the Thirty, From an Old Breton Lay of the Fourteenth Century." *Bentley's Miscellany* 45 (1859): 5–10, 445–59.

> An English translation based on Crapelet's version.

Allmand, C.T., ed. *Society at War: the experience of England and France during the Hundred Years War.* New York: Barnes & Noble Books, 1973.

> One of Froissart's versions of the Combat can be found translated on pp. 124–6.

Le Bel, Jean, *Chronique de Jean le Bel.* Edited by Jules Viard and Eugène Déprez. Paris: Renouard, 1906.

Brush, Henry Raymond. "La Bataille de trente Anglois et de trente Bretons." *Modern Philology* 9 (1911–1912): 511–44.

———. "La Bataille de trente Anglois et de trente Bretons II." *Modern Philology* 10 (1912–1913): 82–136

> The first part comprises Brush's introduction, the second his edition of the two manuscripts with commentary on the text.

Crapelet, G.A., ed. and trans. *Le Combat de trente Bretons contre trente Anglois publié d'après le manuscrit de la Bibliothéque du Roi.* Paris: Crapelet, 1827.

Doyle, Arthur Conan. *Sir Nigel.* 1906; various editions since.

> This is a prequel to Doyle's famous historical novel, *The White Company*. Doyle made his young hero a Combatant. Until recently, this fictional account was probably the most accessible one in English.

Froissart, Jean, *Oeuvres*. Edited by Kervyn de Lettenhove. Translated by Kervyn de Lettenhove, Brussels, 1867–1877.

> Froissart's versions can be found in v. 5, pp. 289–95.

Wyntoun, Androw of. *The Orygynale Cronykil of Scotland.* Edited by David Laing. Edinburgh: Edmonston and Douglas, 1872.

Works on Formal Combats and the Hundred Years War

Barker, Juliet. *The Tournament in England 1100–1400.* Woodbridge: Boydell Press, 1986.

> This excellent survey has a brief discussion of the Combat and similar pre-arranged fights on pp. 158–9

Muhlberger, Steven. *Deeds of Arms: Formal combats in the late fourteenth century.* Union City: Chivalry Bookshelf, 2005.

> Includes a detailed discussion of the various accounts of the Combat.

Strickland, Matthew. "Provoking or Avoiding Battle? Duel and single combat in warfare of the High Middle Ages," in *Armies, Chivalry and Warfare: Proceedings of the 1995 Harlaxton Symposium*, ed. Matthew Strickland. Stamford, Lincolnshire: Paul Watkins, 1998. Pp. 317–43.

> A good introduction to the subject of challenges between enemy champions.

Sumption, Jonathan. *The Hundred Years War.* Vol. 1, *Trial by Battle.* Philadelphia: University of Pennsylvania Press, 1990.

———. *The Hundred Years War.* Vol. 2, *Trial by Fire.* Philadelphia: University of Pennsylvania Press, 1999.

> These two volumes are the best narrative and analysis of the early stages of the war. It provides a detailed account of the Breton wars and discusses the Combat itself in v. 2, pp. 33–5.

Wright, Nicholas. *Knights and Peasants: The Hundred Years War in the French countryside.* Woodbridge: Boydell Press, 1999.

> A somber look at the chaotic nature of the French wars in the fourteenth and fifteenth centuries.